JUST FOR
YOUTH

JUST FOR YOUTH

RICKY ROBERTS III

Just for YOUth
Copyright © 2015 by Ricky Roberts III. All rights reserved.

Interior design by Manolito Bastasa
Cover design by Harbr Co
Bio photo by Dave Brozik

Published in the United States of America

1. Self-Help / General / Teens / Young Adult
2. Self-Help / Personal Growth / Self-Esteem

CONTENTS

INTRODUCTION

———— ◆ ————

THIS BOOK IS written for you, the youth of our world. To be clear and upfront, I am not writing this book to tell you how to live your life. I do not claim to understand what it's like to be you. I don't have all of the answers. I am not perfect. I have made mistakes and will make more.

I write this book for you to share things that have helped me in many aspects of life. Things that I have learned through life and the experiences I have had. I speak to thousands of youth and adults on a yearly basis. I have worked with young people in everything from private schools to maximum-security juvenile detention centers. Despite the experiences and opportunities I have had to speak in various settings to different people, my education, books, etc. I don't really know anything more than you. Yeah, maybe if we get technical, but not really. The truth is I am just another person who grew up with challenges and struggles, which so many of us can relate to. I never imagined being someone that people would care to listen to. When speakers came into my classes, as a teen, I would think they were from a completely different world. For the most part, they never seemed to understand me, and I didn't understand them. To be one of "those" people now trips me out often. I take the opportunity very seriously and am completely humbled by it.

As you read this book, try not to think of it as someone telling you what to be, how to be, and/or how you should live your life. I invite you to think of it more as this: I am sharing little bits of information with you, putting tools in front of you. You get to choose what you want to use, or not, what you like or don't. If there are things you don't agree with or make you feel annoyed, frustrated, or even misunderstood, it is not my intent. Let it be what it is and move on from there. I respect you. I value your opinions, dreams, choices, and efforts to be who you are. I honor the struggles you may have faced or are facing. Thank you for choosing to read this book, written specifically for you. I hope you enjoy it.

This book is dedicated to the youth of our world. Without them, we have no future. May we all take the time to listen to our youth, make the time for them, and open up to the many ways they have to teach us.

LIFE IS ABOUT
MORE THAN MONEY

◆

I KNOW HOW exciting it is to think about "balling," having cars, jewelry, and lots of money. I also appreciate how these things can make you happy, and in some ways they do. I will not deny that truth. However, money and the things it can buy will only be a temporary means to your happiness.

As you move through the next several years of your life, you will be faced with many decisions and have to answer a lot of questions. This is a part of your slow transition into adulthood. As you do, there will be many questions that come up about your career path. In those talks, the subject of money will more than likely come up. It is inevitable. There is a huge amount of pressure to fit in. The people who are most glamorized in our society, generally speaking, are the ones with a lot of money and fancy things.

Again, I acknowledge, it is attractive. It certainly was to me at one time. Fresh out of high school, I wanted to work with youth. I wanted to use my challenges and adversities as a young person to help others. I started junior college to pursue a degree in early childhood development with the intent and plan to finish my Associates of Arts degree, become a director of a before and after school center, which would allow me to make decent money, as I finished college. My thought was to then go onto finish my Bachelors in Education, become a teacher, and get my Masters in Counseling to be a guidance counselor. It was what I felt called to do. Along the way, I bought a used car from the owner of a dealership. I liked him right away. I was eighteen and still seeking a male role model in my life, as my own father was not around at the time, and had not been since I was twelve. It turned out that this man's wife was the guidance counselor at the school I was working at then. Eventually, she started asking me if I would consider working for her husband at the car lot. "He really likes you and wants you to come work for him," she would tell me. Honestly, it felt good to have a positive male person want me to work for him. I would find myself stopping by the dealership to talk with him and his dad often.

I started working for him to pay off a pair of rims he bought for my car. After I paid them off, he started paying me to work on Saturdays. Saturdays then turned into a few days a week. I then left my position at the recreation center to work at the car lot full time. Shortly before I finished my Associates of Arts degree, he offered me a position as sales manager, great pay for my age, and a promise for more advancement as time went on. At that point, I started to experience, for the first time in my life, what it meant to have money and the things I could do and have with it. I chose to turn from my passion to work with youth and go all in at the car lot. (I did still volunteer working with youth in different capacities, here and there.) I was the sales manager, did finance, started buying inventory, became partners, and eventually signed a contract to buy the established name and inventory, along with a fifteen-year lease on the property. I was fully committed. I thought it was my life. My goal was to be somewhat retired by the age of forty-five. I was contractually obligated to over a million dollars for the inventory, lease on the property, and the use of the well-established business name. At the same time, I owned a home, one rental condo and had a contract to buy another one Downtown St. Petersburg. I had good amounts of money in the bank. I was there on paper. Along the way, I had multiple cars, everything from sports cars to SUVs, to luxury touring sedans (most had rims and loud stereo systems). There was actually a time I had a daily driver, a weekend car, and a motorcycle. I was able to buy nice things. So many of the things I believed would make me happy were not. I had stuff. I had expensive jewelry, good investments and a decent amount of money in the bank. I was successful in the eyes of so many, according to societal measures. There were many times I thought to myself, "This is it! I am becoming successful. This is the life and the stuff that will make me happy." As time went on, the ideas of what happiness meant to me started to change. The fulfillment from a different car, all of the time, became less and less. The amount of money I needed to have saved in order to feel good became more and more. If I made one amount of money, it quickly shifted to how I needed to make more. It became about the money. I truly thought that was the thing that made people happy. I thought the ones around me growing up with money were happy because of it. The musicians, movie stars, performers, etc., on TV, radio, the Internet, and in the papers seem to be so happy with their money and things. I was driven to succeed. I was focused to become a millionaire. I thought that would be my happiness.

As I realized, more and more I was not being fulfilled, I was also losing money at the same time. Eventually, I walked away from the business. I lost thousands of dollars, sold my rental condo, and ended up essentially bankrupt, with very little in regards to material things. I went from driving virtually any car I wanted to driving a 1987 Honda Accord and a motor scooter. Through it all, pursuing my passion to write and creating *You Are Valued* (a nonprofit organization that inspires young people, all people for that matter, to see the value in who they are and appreciate the same in others) I have found it's truly not about the money; it is about being happy. Do I think money is important? Absolutely. Do we need it to sustain? For sure. Is it nice to have a lot of it? Most definitely. Are fancy cars and big houses nice? Of course. Do I intend to make good amounts of money, again? Sure thing, but only if it is made with pursuing my passion and things that truly matter to me.

Please listen (read) closely. You will need money to participate in our society, no mater what you think or feel about it. There is no way around that. Having more than enough money does make things easier in certain regards. Very important! As you are choosing what you want to do with your life, I encourage you to not let money be the main deciding factor. Is it necessary to consider? Yes, but remember there is so much more to your life than money. Pursue the things that matter. The things that make you feel alive. Inspire you. Drive you to become better. Maybe those pursuits won't earn you much money at first or much at all compared to what some high-paying jobs will. That's okay. If they make you happy, if you feel like life wouldn't be right without it, and/or it inspires you when you awake and motivates you as you're going to sleep, then it's worth more than anything money can ever buy you.

The truth is you can have millions upon millions of dollars, but if you're not happy with who you are and the life you're living and feeling content with how you're earning the money, then it is worth nothing at all. The ultimate goal in life is to enjoy it, to be happy, and to live a passion and purpose-filled life. It's okay to go for making *big money*, a.k.a. to be "ballin," just don't let it be the only thing that motivates you. In the end, you will be remembered more for the way you lived your life, how you made others feel, and the people you helped along the way than how much money you made.

Do the things you love and the money will come!

Reflect:

What are at least three things that motivate you?

What are three things that make you feel happy?

Where do you get your inspiration?

What does your dream life look like?

What are some other thoughts and ideas that are coming to you after reading this section?

NOT EVERYONE HAS TO LIKE YOU

THERE IS A lot of pressure on you. Questions are asked like: What do you want to be when you grow up? Will you go to college? Which one? Who are you? What music defines you? What is your sexual orientation? On top of the many questions you get and ask yourself, you also have demands. Stay out of trouble. Go to school. Get good grades. Figure out who you are, and what you want to do with your life. Then there is pressure. The pressure from your peer groups to fit in. To be somebody. To be cool. Wanted. Accepted. Liked. Interesting. Well dressed. Impressive. Important. Pretty. Cute. Hot. Fit. Popular.

Before I go any further, I want you to know how much I respect you. I appreciate the efforts you have made to be who you are today, right now. I know life is not easy.

I especially know it's not easy to be a youth at this time in our existence. You are faced with more demands, distractions, pressures, and others being cruel more than ever. I commend you!

You are valued for who you are and who you will continue to become.

Thank you for choosing to spend your time reading this far into the book. I hope it's reaching you well.

Okay, back to it. As much as you may want to be liked by everyone, you will not be. Yes, that is right. Even the most popular, famous people are not liked by everyone. I am sure you get that by what you witness through gossip. You may be saying, "I know that already." I imagine you do and am glad for that. Now, I encourage you to go beyond knowing it and feeling it. You don't have to fit in to anyone's group. You don't have to be invited to every activity, party or to be surrounded by large amounts of people to be "somebody." You are already somebody just as you are. Whether no one likes you or many people do, none of that is what defines you.

I was asked to give a closing talk at a training event for teachers, school social workers, behavior specialists, and other direct service staff. The coordinator of the event wanted me to inspire the group to see the value in the great work they do. I assured her that I would do my best. My talk focused on thanking them for the difference they make in our world and the importance of their work. The response from the audience was great! I got an e-mail a week later with the evaluations each attendee filled out for my talk. I felt inspired as I read through them one by one. People were saying a lot of really nice things. However, as I read through the stack of several hundred evaluations, I came across one that was not so good. The person gave me all low scores and even wrote, "Don't quit your day job." I was a bit humbled and on some levels hurt. I quickly reminded myself that not everyone will like me; they don't have to. I then thought in reference to his comment: it's too late, I already quit my "day job."

I spent many years of my life with the pressure of wanting everyone to like me. When I realized it is impossible literally, I became much more comfortable with being myself. If people don't like me for me, then simply put, they just don't like me. It doesn't mean I am right and they are wrong, it just means they don't like me. I can't live my life hoping everyone will like me. I have to live it knowing I like myself. In truth, I still deal with wanting everyone to like me, what I write, the talks I give, and do put pressure on myself, but I remind myself of the same things I am sharing with you.

On that note, keep in mind that I have struggles like we all do. Just because I share this stuff with you doesn't mean I don't lose my focus and direction at times. I want you to know, I am a person doing my best just like you.

I have found that if you live for everyone to like you, you will not fully learn to like yourself, which is the most important of all. Not everyone will like you. Find peace in the reality of it. There is nothing wrong with you. At the end of the day, for those who don't like you, it's their loss for missing out on being friends with someone as great as *you*.

Don't create your life around what you think will make everyone like you. Do it around what will make you like/ love yourself.

Reflect:

Name three positive things about yourself.

What are three accomplishments that you have made in your life? How did it make you feel when you made them?

Why do you think it's important to like/love yourself?

Are there any other thoughts, feelings, or ideas that are coming to you?

MISTAKES ARE OKAY

I HAVE MADE mistakes in my life and can imagine I will make more. There were many times when I condemned myself really bad for them. One mistake that comes to mind at the moment is "burning up" the motor on my motor scooter. I was in the middle of finishing up my bachelor of arts degree, releasing my fourth book, *Awakening the New You: A Path to Transformation*, and starting "You Are Valued." My mind was all over the place. I knew the oil was running low in my scooter and that I needed to put some in it. Even though I knew it, I kept forgetting. I had a pretty far ride to do a final presentation for my degree and told myself I need to put more oil in before I go. I was running late for the presentation and completely forgot. As I was cruising along, the scooter made a loud noise and stopped running instantly. I burned up the motor from not putting oil in it when I knew it was low.

Fortunately, I had a friend nearby that was able to give me a ride to the college to present my final project. As far as the scooter goes, I had to get the entire motor rebuilt, which cost over six hundred dollars. I got real down on myself for letting the mistake of not taking five minutes to put oil in my scooter cause me to spend money I didn't really have to spend at that time. I know better than to run anything low on oil, but I made a mistake and had to let it go. I had to remind myself that there was nothing more I could do but be kind to myself and learn my lesson about not taking enough time to take care of the many details of my life. Burning up the motor in my scooter made me look at the business of my life at the time and how out of balance I was. The mistake I made with my scooter was a great reminder to me on many levels.

Often times, through out our lives, we are scolded and disciplined for our mistakes. Sometimes we are made to feel that we are not allowed to make them. We are guilted, judged, and, at times, forgotten because of them. The truth is, anyone who has given you a hard time, or is, about your mistakes, judging you, making you feel less than the awesome person you are, have all made mistakes too. I am as guilty as anyone for judging others by their mistakes.

However, as guilty as I may be, I know I have no right, especially when I look at my own life and some of the choices that I have made to judge anyone or make them feel bad for the mistakes they have made.

It's okay to make mistakes. Part of learning is done through the mistakes we make. Don't beat yourself up about the mistakes that you have made (don't beat yourself at all really). Do your best to let them go. You can't do anything to change them now no matter how much you may want to. It may be that some of your mistakes are things that people know you for. Maybe they are even things that people give you a hard time for. I wish I could say something to change that and get people to see those mistakes are just that, mistakes, and everyone makes them at one time or another. I would also want them to see they are only a small part of who you are. Unfortunately, there will be people who only see you for your mistakes. There may even be things you want to pursue that will meet resistance because of them. Don't let any of it discourage you. Let me be clear: none of this is to suggest that you should not have any regard for your choices and put them off as, "Oh well, they are just mistakes, and everyone makes them." Regardless of that truth, we still have to be our best. Be accountable. Ultimately, you have to realize that some mistakes can stick with you for a lifetime. If that is the case, again, your mistakes don't define you in your fullness. The more you learn from them and try not to make the same mistakes over and over again, the better you will become because of them. What your mistakes were as a child compared to what they are now and versus what they may be in the future, are likely different. What ever they are or have been, seek growth from them. Look for ways to be better. Be kind to yourself. Be honest with yourself, and others. Always remember you will make mistakes. It's okay; everyone does. It's not the mistakes that define you; it's what you do with them.

Beyond the mistakes that you may have made and/ or will make, no matter how big or small they were/are, you will always have the potential to do amazing things, if you choose.

You are destined for greatness!

Reflect:

What have you learned from certain mistakes that you have made? How can you use it to grow as a person?

Why do you think it's important to learn from your mistakes?

What does "You are destined for greatness" mean to you?

Is there anything else that you would like add or share?

DON'T BURN BRIDGES

I AM SURE that I have burned bridges along the way and some of them have been from mistakes I have made. I have done things that have hurt people to the point where it may not be welcomed for me to cross over that bridge again. Although I have done my best not to do that, it has happened. I am also certain that people I have hurt when I was much younger through unnecessary acts of violence and/or not handling relationships with as much love and kindness as they should be would not want me to cross their bridge. If I could apologize to every person I have ever made feel less than valued, I certainly would. I am not perfect, nor will I ever claim to be. Even though I have burned bridges, there are many more I have not. I have done my best for the biggest part of my life not to burn a bridge, as I never know when I need to cross it again. In other words, you never know when the people in your life will leave it, or you leave theirs, but then cross paths again with them in the future. Only time will tell if you will need them, or they may you. Let me be clear. This is not trying to get everyone to like you. People don't have to like you to be able to cross that bridge. People not liking you is much different than you wronging them so much that they not only don't like you, but will close the door in your face, if you came to it. No one wants that.

As you move through your life many things will change. You will continue to move forward. Even when you make mistakes, hurt others, if you do your best to be respectful and act with integrity, you will not burn bridges. As time passes, things will heal and change. You may have hurt someone, but you will still have the bridge to cross again when needed.

Maybe this doesn't seem important to you or just simply isn't. However, it will someday. Tell people the truth. Be mindful of how your thoughts, words, and actions make others feel. Do your best to make good on mistakes you make, especially when they hurt others. Be authentic. When you do cross paths with people from your past, and you will. It will feel good to know those bridges were not burned.

Think of your name (or the name you go by) as your own brand, like Van's, Apple, Nike, Tom's, Hurley, etc. Everything you say, do, share, post on Facebook, Instagram, Twitter, and act on is a representation of your brand. The question is, what do you want your brand to be best known for? You get to choose to make your brand be one that others will remember and welcome with open arms when they see it—you.

You are your own brand, and your brand is special. Take care of it!

Reflect:

What do you want to be known as and remembered for?

If you had to come up with a slogan (i.e., "I live to inspire others.") that helps define you, what would it be?

What does it mean to be authentic?

Is there anything else you feel inspired to add?

MAKE NICE COOL

◆

IT IS NOT a secret that being mean is not only accepted; it has become cool. It is common and perceived to be okay to humiliate people, to call them names, and to hurt them. As a society, we continue to make it okay. The problem I have with that is, people are dying because of it. People say, "Sticks and stones may break my bones, but names never hurt me." Whoever thought that was true is wrong. That's what I grew up hearing. I also use to hurt others. I laughed at people being hurt, and I got encouraged when I hurt others by my peers. Everything from calling names to beating people up to the point of blood sprinkling on my clothes, I did it. I didn't think being nice was the "cool thing to do." In fact, it was cooler to be mean, hurtful, violent, and angry than it was to be nice.

Unfortunately, I feel like that's still the case today. People are able to take being mean to a whole new level and do it more frequently because of the lack of face-to-face accountability through social media. The thing that really gets me is people are dying because of the way people are treating them. People are being tormented and hurt so much that they are taking their own lives. Now, imagine if you and many others chose to make being nice cool. What if being nice was the new cool thing to do? What if as a society we gave as much attention to those who are nice as we do to the ones who are not? As an individual, you can make nice cool. Beyond just being nice to your friends and family, you can also be nice to your peers, teachers, custodians, lunch room staff, younger children, store clerks, strangers, etc. You can keep being you and just be nice. You can encourage others when they are nice. Most importantly, you can choose not to laugh or encourage behavior that is not nice, aka bullying, in any way. In fact, you can choose to make it less cool by saying, "Hey, that's not cool."

You may be thinking, "That won't work. I am only one person." I say what if young people read this all over the world and you choose to make nice cool, and thousands, if not millions, of others decide to do the same. What if you shared this with a class or group and suggest that everyone should read this chapter? Then imagine everyone who reads this decides to make nice cool. Imagine how great it would be at school, parties, on teams, or in groups if everyone was nice to one another.

None of us like what it feels like to be disrespected, called names, hurt, or put down. If not one of us like it, then it's time to make it stop. It's not cool to make others feel bad about who they are or what they may be experiencing in their life. You can change that one person at a time. You can make nice cool. It's pretty simple, be nice, and encourage others to do the same. In fact, just by choosing to be nice yourself, you will naturally inspire others to do the same.

I will guarantee you this, and I don't guarantee much, your life will be less stressful, happier, and more productive if you choose to make nice cool. Thank you for making a difference with me.

Reflect:

How do you feel about the way you treat others?

Have you ever been lied to, disrespected, mistreated, put down, or hurt at any point in your life? Name one. Did you like it?

Have you ever done something nice for someone? How did it feel to you?

Who is one person in your life you can choose to start being nicer to?

Do people feel lifted up or put down when they are around you?

BE YOUR BEST

BEFORE I BEGIN, it's important to point out that everyone's best is different and we should appreciate that about one another. What your best is may be much different from what mine is as mine could be much different from yours. For example, my best at building something may be a room, and someone else's best could be building an entire house. Your best in math may be getting a *B*, but your best in art is an *A*. On that same note, another person's best at art could be a *C* but an *A* in math. The most important thing is to do our best at whatever we choose to do. No one else knows what your best is like you do. If you're honest with yourself, you will know if you are truly doing your best, what ever that is, and at what ever you do. Other people can have an idea of what your best is, set standards for you, but ultimately you are the one who knows better than anyone, and you choose to operate at that capacity or not.

It's not about getting the highest score, being the fastest, smartest, richest, coolest, prettiest, or funniest; it's about giving everything you do your best. This world is waiting for you. You have talents, insights, and gifts that only you can share. When you are being your best, you are allowing the world to benefit from your many reasons to be here at all.

Set your standards high. Pursue your passions, interests, talents, and dreams. Enjoy time with your family, friends, and peers. What ever it is you do, do it your best. No matter how much I grow or how much I excel at something, I believe there is always room for improvement. By knowing I am doing my best, the desire to raise the bar occurs naturally. Again, your bar and room for improvement is unique to you despite how similar it may appear to be to others.

When talking about being your best, I think it's also important to recognize that being your best applies to all areas of your life. It's not just about being your best in school, in your hobbies, your passions, and creative expression; it's about being your best as a person, in the relationships, and interactions you have with the individuals around you. Whether it is your relationships, friendships, or interactions with strangers, give them your best.

When you are being your best, not only will the world smile because of it, you will smile at yourself, which ultimately is most important.

Thank you for being your best! You deserve it!

Reflect:

What is something you are really good at? Are you doing your best?

Name three areas of your life that you can do better at.

How do you feel when you know in your heart that you are doing your very best at something?

Who is someone in your life that inspires you to be your best? (Don't take that person for granted in your life, as people who inspire you to be your best are very important.)

What is something that you can do to inspire others to be their best?

YOU DON'T HAVE TO BE
GOOD AT EVERYTHING

THIS IS A bit of an extension of the previous chapter: always do your best. In the mindset of always doing your best, it is important to bring up that it's okay if you're not good at everything; you don't have to be. If everyone was good at everything, I am not sure the world would be nearly as exciting as it is.

A big part of what makes us each so great is that our strengths are different; in the same way, our best is different.

Have you ever felt pressured to be good at everything you try or do? I have.

Have you ever avoided trying something new because you were afraid you would not be good at it? I have done that too. I have always loved art! I grew up drawing and still do. I always appreciated painting as well but never did it because of the pressure I put on myself to be good at everything. I was afraid I wouldn't be good at it. Although I did random paintings in high school, I still didn't paint as much as I really wanted to. Eventually I decided that I don't have to be "good" at it to do it. As long as I try my best and enjoy it, then I should paint. My painting is not on the same skill level as my drawing is, but I love the way I feel when I do it, which ultimately is most important.

I respect the pressure you may feel to be good at everything, and even the desire to be so. I acknowledge that it may come from friends, teachers, family members, peers, yourself, and/or society in general. Quite honestly, there will always be people who pressure you. One thing to be most concerned with, however, is how much pressure you put on yourself.

Are you hard on yourself? If so, why? What makes you feel like you have to be good at everything? I can almost guarantee you that there are things that you are good at that some of your favorite people, most liked athletes, actors/actresses, and/or musicians are not good at all. As you learn of the things that you are good at and not so good at, be kind to yourself. Life will give you enough to worry about. You will feel pressure in many different ways and capacities in your life; that's reality. Don't create extra pressure and stress in your life or put yourself down because of an illusion that you have to be good at everything you do.

Be kind to yourself. You are awesome! You have many gifts and talents to share with the world. Just remember: it's okay if you're not good at everything; you don't have to be.

Reflect:

Do you put unnecessary pressure on yourself to be good at everything? Why do you think that is?

Do you think it's possible to be good at everything?

Name at least three things that you are good at.

Name at least three things that you are not good at. Are you okay with that?

What are three things you would like to try but are afraid of not being good at them? Try them!

BE YOURSELF

YOU HAVE INFORMATION coming at you from many angles. Be this way, it will make you cool. If you get accepted into that group, you'll be important. If you act this way or have these shoes, this haircut, this style or that one, people will like you. If you are good at this sport or are in a band, people will really like you. The list of messages that you get from social media, television, magazines, music, and/or your peers is huge. It doesn't seem to stop. Believe me, adult's deal with it too. I can appreciate how overwhelming the needs to fit in so many different ways can be.

As a speaker in a variety of settings, I often feel the pressure to be someone I am not. For example, when I speak at national conferences, I feel the pressure to dress a certain way. The voice in my head says, "I am the keynote speaker. Should I wear a suit? Everyone will be dressed up. Will they take me less serious if I am not dressed up?" It goes on and on. No one ever tells me specifically what to wear. It's something I put on myself because I know that most everyone else will be in a suit or dressy attire of some sort. The truth is I am not myself when I wear a suit, or a button up dress shirt. I don't feel comfortable. I am myself when I wear a nice pair of pants, a shirt with out a collar, and a pair of Vans classics. Have I had people make comments about my dress? Yes. Do I let it bother me? Not really. I have a solution that will make it easier for you to enjoy life, and to not be so bothered by what group you fit into, or not. It is to be yourself. Ultimately, when I am myself, I am the most inspired, and in return, people will get the best I have to give.

Yes, it is that simple. Be you. I spent many years of my life being someone I was not. There are still times that I fall into the pressure of being a certain way to be liked or accepted. The years that I was the most angry and confused in my life were the years that I was not comfortable with being myself. I laughed at jokes that I didn't think were funny. I did things I didn't really care to do. I fought people, and even hurt friends, just because I wanted to be liked. I didn't think I was enough to be liked for being myself, not who others wanted me to be. As time went on, the more comfortable I became with myself, the more enjoyable life became. Being around people became easier, when I felt confident enough to truly be myself.

Be honest with who you are, what you like, or don't like. When you are yourself and comfortable with who you are, it doesn't matter who likes you or doesn't. Ultimately, the friends and people you really want in your life are the one's who like you for you, not who they want you to be. Not to mention, if you are not true to yourself, it's too much work to pretend, and to be someone you're not. What fun is that? It's not fun at all actually. It's work. It's tiring and even confusing. It's also not being real. For example, don't pretend to like a certain band because other people do or enjoy sports because it will make you fit in; like them because it's who you are. Do things because you enjoy them, not because you feel like it will make you cool if you do. Life is not easy. People are not always nice. Find your peace with that. Don't live to get acceptance from others, live to be the person you are just as you are. The best *you* that you can ever be is *yourself*.

You are not only enough; you are more than enough.

Reflect:

Name three things that make you who you are.

Name three of your greatest qualities.

Why do you think it's important to be yourself?

What does it mean to you when I said, "You are not only enough, you are more than enough?"

SET GOALS

As you read this section, please keep in mind this is about your goals, not mine or anyone else's. I am not going to tell you what goals to set or even how to set them. I want to simply talk with you about how helpful they are and have been to me. My books, creating "You Are Valued," and the opportunities I have to speak to thousands of people on a yearly basis happen because of setting goals and taking action to achieve them. Goals are something that gives us a result to work toward, a focus if you will. A goal can be set on anything from learning a new trick on a skateboard to opening up a dance studio.

I personally put my goals in different categories. There are ones that I consider short term, which are not too far out from the present; long term, which could be a year, or more; down the road; and ultimate, which are the bigger and overall visions of my life (what I am ultimately working toward). The time in which you complete a goal is not as important, at least to me, as having them and taking action toward reaching them. Have time ranges to focus on and push to reach them, but don't get caught up on them too much. Yes, set realistic times to reach your goals, but don't get overly stressed when it takes longer than desired, and/or planned. The truth is, there will always be things that happen, changes that arise, and obstacles that occur that will interfere with your projected times of completion. These are important parts of the process in reaching your goals.

Why are goals important?

Goals give you direction. They help you visualize and think of things that you want to achieve in your life. Again, things *you* want to achieve in *your* life.

Write them down!

When you write them down it's like saying this is what I will do. Then when you get to check them off, it is an empowering experience. I am purposely not giving you directions and more descriptions about types of goals and how to set them because I want you to be encouraged to find ways that work well for you. I did, however, include a short activity for you at the end of this section. You can actually use it over and over again as you accomplish goals if you choose.

Think about the things that are important to you, that make you happy. Passions you have. Ways you want to improve your life. Some may be things you can change now, and some may be things that will take time and a lot of work to reach. You will know the difference. You will know which goals work for you and how to make them happen. Also, when you write down your goals, consider writing down actions you can take right now toward reaching them. It takes hard work, dedication, sacrifice, and action to achieve your goals. Your goals will not be accomplished just because you write them down and/or talk about them. They will only be reached if you take action on them. Moreover, be mindful of the people and/or things that may be distracting you from reaching your goals. You have to ask yourself, "How much do I want to reach my goals and are they worth avoiding the things that distract me from them?"

Goals are a great tool to keep you moving toward being your best and making the most of the gifts and talents you've been given. Your goals may be very different from others, and that's okay. The most important thing is that you set them and, above all, that you take actions toward achieving them.

You are destined to do great things!

Reflect:

What are three short-term goals you have? Long-term? Ultimate?

Write down three things that can distract you from reaching them. What will help you achieve them?

What are actions that you can take right now toward reaching your goals?

CHOOSE YOUR
FRIENDS WISELY

YOU MAY NOT get to choose your family, but you do get to choose your friends. Although your family may encourage you to stay away from certain people and/or certain groups, for the most part (parents don't cringe), you will still hang out with who you want. If you like someone, or love them, in most cases, you won't take the advice of others telling you not to spend time with them. I get that. I certainly am not one that likes people telling me what I can or cannot do.

Think about what you want out of life. What is important to you? What causes do you care about? Do your friends, and/or your girl friend / boyfriend support who you really are? Do they inspire you? Do they motivate you to pursue your dreams? Do they encourage you to be your best? Do they respect you, and your decisions? Do they have goals of their own? What do they want out of life? These questions are important to consider in regard to the company you keep. Your friends, or people you choose to spend your time with, don't need to have the same views, ideas, and direction as you do but should certainly support you in yours. Naturally, it's great when they do. When you choose to spend time with people who don't care about your direction, or their own for that matter, they will distract you. They will bring you down. Although they may not make you do bad things or keep you from being great yourself, it is best not to choose people in your life who are weighing you down versus lifting you up. Life is hard enough. You have too many amazing things to do then to get brought down by others.

There will be people you really care about who make bad choices. It may get to the point where you need to create space between you and them. This is hard. Believe me, I have had to do this with more than one long time friend. One of my younger sisters passed away several years ago. She died from an oxycodone overdose. I was working to find my peace in the experience. At the same time, I had one my best friends, Rob, who was struggling with addiction. On top of the pain of losing my sister and going through the grieving process, I couldn't stand to watch a close friend ruin his life. Although I love him very much, I was losing respect for who he was at the time because of how he was choosing to live his life. Eventually I had to

create space from him. It was hard. I wanted to help h
but knew he had to be ready to help himself. He was
ready for change then, and I couldn't let it bring me dow
I would still reach out to let him know I cared but spe
very little time with him. He knew I loved him and why
was keeping my distance. He also knew that I believed i
him and was there for him from a distance. Rob is doing
amazing now.

It's not easy to let go of people who are not positive
additions to your life, but it's not best for you or them when
you hold on. Sometimes people need to lose great friends
before they wake up to the changes they need to make to
live their fullest potential. This does not mean you are not
caring or loyal. It doesn't make you mean or stuck up. It is
okay to let go of people who are not good for you. You can
still have love for them and even be there for them, even if
it is done from a distance.

You are amazing! I encourage you to choose people t
be in your life who appreciate your greatness and are doin
their best to live their fullest potential as you are.

Reflect:

Do your closest friend encourage you? Support you? Insp
you? Explain how.

Are there any friends that may be distracting you from being your best? How do they distract you?

Why do you think it's important to surround yourself with positive people?

STAY FOCUSED

$\Longleftrightarrow$

DON'T WORRY. I am not about to tell you not to have fun and that you have to be serious all of the time. That is not the case at all. I am simply encouraging you to keep your attention focused and to be mindful of the choices you make and how they impact your life.

Focus on the things that are important to you. If you don't have anything that you feel inspired to stay focused on, I invite you to find something. The result of staying focused on things that matter to you is a continued expansion of your gifts, talents, and strengths.

I have made many bad choices. As a young person, I was constantly on the verge of really hurting someone or doing something destructive that could have gotten me into a lot of trouble. Although this was the case, I believe I would have been even worse off with my choices, and maybe even dead if I didn't have my attention so focused on skateboarding. The trouble that I caused and got into was done in very few hours in comparison to how many I spent skateboarding. In other words, my focus on skateboarding consumed most of my time. Even time I was not actually skating, I was still focused on it. I would imagine the new tricks I wanted to learn, the stairs I wanted to do, and/or the video footage I wanted to get. The point is, my focus on skateboarding saved my life. I can only imagine how much more trouble I would have gotten into with all the free time I would have had without it. Overall, skateboarding helped me in all areas of my life.

It's no secret; we are living in crazy times. You have a lot of distractions. You have peer pressure from so many sides and angles. Stay focused on who you are and on the things that matter to you, things that you're passionate about. It's also important to stay focused on your friends, family, relationships, your growth as an individual, and learning.

People, things, and/or experiences will hurt you. Life will happen, and when it does, you have to stay focused.

When things get crazy, when you feel like giving up, hold on, check in, and stay focused.

When people are telling you that you can't do something or you're not good enough, stay focused on the belief you have in yourself.

When you feel like giving up on anything, stay focused on your strengths, hold it together, keep your head up, and keep pushing on. Stay focused!

Above all, stay focused on being the outstanding and amazing person you are.

Reflect:

What are three things that you are focused on?

What is something that being focused helped you accomplish?

What are three areas of your life that could benefit from you being more focused?

HAVE COMPASSION

COMPASSION IS HAVING concern and awareness for, and of, others, including but not limited to their troubles, pains, heartaches, and/or circumstances. It is also the desire to help. There are many reason and examples I can give of ways to be compassionate, but I will leave those to you as I am sure you have many great ones.

Despite the examples we give, the reality is they can be seen around us every day. I encourage you to consider that everyone you see with problems are people too. Although they may be different, they are still people. Never think that what ever their problems are that they would never happen to you or someone you know. We are all susceptible to any of life's problems, illnesses, and/or challenges as much as the next person is.

People are hurting all around us, and we don't always know it. Think about the many people you pass on a daily basis who may be hurting, and you don't know it. Think of the people who appear to be okay on the outside, the ones who smile every day. The ones that everyone would think are perfectly happy.

Have you ever been going through something hard, hurting inside, but made it appear to the outside world that everything was okay? We all do it. We carry our pain, hide it, and cover it up with fake smiles. I remember times in high school when the water and electric at the house I lived was shut off because of my mom's inability to pay the bill. When we had no running water, I would take a "shower" behind my house before school with a gallon of water that I would buy at a local convenient store. You can't use much soap when you only have one gallon of water to get clean with. I didn't always smell the best. I would cringe inside when people would smell my body odor and start asking, "Who stinks?" I would always hope that people didn't realize it was me that didn't smell good. I felt so ashamed. Isolated. Alone. The people around me never knew how I felt inside because of the fake smiles I would put on and the image of being "tuff" I hid behind. Now, think about those times when you were hurting and no one knew and someone did something hurtful to you. Did it make you feel worse than you already did? I am guessing it did. Imagine if the person that was hurtful was more compassionate and kind to you. The idea is to be mindful of the reality that all of us are going through something at one time or another and on one level or another. Be compassionate for what others may be going through, even if they don't tell you or you don't see it. Care for them as individuals, and respect that the journey of life isn't necessarily an easy one for any of us.

Imagine this: I am carrying a backpack. In that backpack, I have bricks. Those bricks represent the emotional weight I carry inside. When something else happens that doesn't feel good, more bricks are put into my bag. As I am going through my life, the bag keeps filling up. Then one day someone does something hurtful to me. My bag is too heavy. I can't handle the weight of any more bricks in my bag. I have to let it go. Quit carrying it. I drop the bag. This is what happens to people who take their life. They can't keep going. They give up. The weight is too heavy. The reality is when you are compassionate for others you can take weight out of their bag. Now, on the other side, by not being compassionate of other people's situations or feelings, you can put extra weight in someone's bag. At any point, you do something mean to someone, you are putting a brick in their bag, and for some, it could be the last brick that goes in it, pushing them to the point of dropping it— taking their life. It could be the one brick that makes their bag too heavy to hold. It could be the first time you have ever seen them and/or did something mean to them, but it was the last time it needed to happen.

I mean really think about that. Imagine the people that are around you in your family, neighborhood, and school. By being more compassionate, you can not only help them, and/or make their day; you could potentially save their life. On the other side, you could essentially take it by being mean.

Every time I say that or even think of it, it motivates me to be more mindful about how I treat others every day.

I encourage you to ask yourself, "What is it like for people to be on the other side of me?" In other words, what are you putting into the world? Are you putting more kindness and compassion into it or more pain and suffering? The beauty is, you get to decide who you want to be in this world and how you want to be thought of. I invite you to consider how much better the world would be if more people choose to be compassionate versus mean and hurtful. What do you choose?

Reflect:

What does compassion mean to you?

When was a time in your life that you helped someone by being compassionate for him or her?

Have you ever heard of someone committing suicide because they were bullied (people not being kind or compassionate to them)? How did it make you feel?

THERE IS NO HURRY TO GROW UP

I REMEMBER BEING a teenager thinking, I can't wait to turn sixteen so I can drive, eighteen so I can get into clubs, etc. I remember being in high school not being able to wait until I got out. There was always an age or something I was in the hurry to have happen. I was in a hurry to grow up. I wanted a car. I wanted a job so I could buy a car, and other things of course. I wanted to graduate high school so I could be an adult.

Looking back now, I can see where I could have missed out on some amazing experiences as a youth because of the many ways I was in a hurry to grow up. The truth is: there is no need to be in a hurry at all.

Enjoy this time of your life (what ever time it may be). Have goals for your future. Be excited about the freedom that comes from driving. Get motivated by the thought of graduating high school or college. Have direction for you future but don't miss out on enjoying what could be some of the best years of your life.

The world is waiting for you and the many amazing things you will accomplish. It's not going anywhere. Be where you are now. Make the most of it. Have fun. Make friends. Try new things. Explore. Be adventurous. Express who you are and the things that inspire you.

Again, I am not implying not to have future direction. I am not suggesting for you to not be responsible or have no regard for your future, or chosen career path. The point being, you have an entire life in front of you. You will do great things! It is important to actively act upon them. Be productive. Be focused. Set goals. Look forward to your future, but enjoy every step along the way.

Whatever your future holds or doesn't hold, try not to let thoughts of the future keep you from enjoying your life in the now. Cherish being young (or any age you are for that matter) and the perks that come with it. No matter how old you will become (none of us can ever predict just how long we will be here), you will only be every age you are once. There are no do overs. Make the most of your life, and don't rush the process.

There is no hurry to be anywhere other than where you are now. Enjoy every moment of your life, and remember you are only the age you are now once.

Reflect:

Are you enjoying your life now?

Are there things you are trying to rush or in a hurry to make happen?

What is one of your most favorite memories in the past year?

What are three things about your life right now that you really like?

DO YOUR BEST NOT TO JUDGE OTHERS

THE REALITY IS we all judge others on one level or another. Sometimes, we don't even know we are doing it. It just happens. We look at others and think we know something about them or think of the reasons why we are better. This is bound to happen on one level or another. Is it right? No. Does it happen? Yes. The truth is, you and I don't have the right to judge anyone. If you look at someone, the only thing you see is his or her surface; nothing else. You may get a slight idea of who someone could be by the car they are driving, the clothes they are wearing, their gender, sexual orientation, or the shade of their skin, but you won't know them. Sometimes, what you think you know about people by their surface is completely different than who they really are beneath it.

Think about a time someone judged you. Maybe it was because of the clothes you wear, your grades, and/or the sport you play or art you perform. How did it make you feel to be judged? Have you ever wished people would get to know you and not judge you based on what they think they know about you?

Several years ago, I decided to grow a beard. It got super burly. People who didn't know me treated me completely different just because of my beard. A picture of me with a beard, and without one, was actually used by a program called Peace Makers to talk with elementary youth about diversity. The facilitators would show young people and ask them to share what they thought about the people in the photos. When they saw the photo of me without a beard, they would say I was a teacher, counselor, someone nice, etc. When groups saw the photo of me with a beard, they would say I looked like a homeless person, drug dealer, terrorist, and was mean, etc. The only difference in the two photos was in one I had a beard and the other I didn't. The judgments about who the young people thought I was changed based on my appearance alone. People have judged me as I have judged them. Although I did my best to not take the judgment I felt from my beard, personally, it still didn't feel good. Above all, it bothers me to realize how much as a society we still judge one another on the surface as much as we do.

As I mentioned earlier, no one is perfect. You will judge people. I will judge people. My intention is to encourage you to try your best not to. Give people a chance to show you who they are before you decide who you think they are and whether or not you should be friends with them or how to treat them. Give yourself and others the chance to get to know their story. Try to look past whether they are straight or not, their skin color and heritage, the clothes they wear, the color they dye their hair, if they are homeless, or not, what job they have, etc.

It does none of us any good to judge one another. You owe it to yourself, to others, to the world, to try your best not to judge and encourage those around you to do the same.

Thank you for doing your best. Thank you for caring about how you make others feel. Thank you for being you. Whatever you have or don't have, your skin color, mistakes you have made, the clothes you wear, the music you like, or your sexual orientation is, I appreciate you just the same. I respect you and have no judgment on who you are. Shine on!

Reflect:

What have you felt judged for? Did you like it?

What is an example of a time you judged someone and they proved you wrong once you got to know them?

What impact do you think it has on the world when we judge one another?

Do you judge others? If so, do you think you can do better not to? How?

BE GRATEFUL

IT IS EASY to get caught up on thinking about how your life would be better if you lived in a bigger house, had nicer clothes, or even had different people in your life.

Everywhere you look, you are being told what will make you cool, important, or popular. There is influence—generally speaking, to feel like you never have enough and to not only want more but get more. It's okay to want nice things. It's okay to be upset with your family and/or people in your life and to want different ones. The key is to not focus so much on what you want that you forget to be grateful for what you do have right now.

Don't take anything you have or people in your life for granted. Chances are whatever you have, even if it feels like you have very little, is more than others may have. An experience I had comes to mind. I was driving my motor scooter to attend a training about providing special services to youth-based programs in the community. Not only was I running late, but it started to rain. I was feeling discouraged to not have a car at that time, especially when not too many years before I was driving different luxury cars often. I was focusing more on what I didn't have instead of what I did. A man passed in front of me on a bike. He only had one leg but was pedaling along just fine. I thought, *Wow.* Here I am feeling bummed about not having a car, and this guy is pedaling his bike with only one leg.

The light turned green. I proceeded toward my destination. I instantly shifted my focus on the reality that I have so much to be grateful for, even my scooter. Then as I drove forward, I saw a man walking on the sidewalk. I knew he was heading to the same place as me. At that point, the training started in five minutes, and it would have taken him at least fifteen minutes to make it there by walking. I stopped to ask if he wanted a ride. He smiled big as if I was picking him up in a limo and said, "Sure!" We made it to the training on time. He kept thanking me over and over again. He was certainly more than grateful.

All that you have may be everything that someone else only wishes they had. If you are upset with your family, wanting them to be different, remember there are some people that have no family at all. Chances are, for those people, they can only wish they had a family to complain about. No matter how hard your life may seem or be, someone has experienced a lot worse. None of this is to discount your desires and/or frustrations. I simply want to encourage you to be grateful.

Be grateful for the bed you sleep in at night, the people who are in your life (no matter how few they may be), the food you eat, the clothes you wear, the running water you brush your teeth with every day, the physical abilities you have (even if they are limited), and the ability to read this book. Above all, be grateful that you have the opportunity to be here.

There is nothing in this life that is guaranteed except being born and passing on when ever your time may be to do so. You have no warning when this time may be. It just is and will happen with or without your permission. People will come and go. Things will come and go. Your life will continue to change. When you are overwhelmed, stressed out with life or sad, switch your focus to being grateful for the many gifts in your life. When you start looking at reasons to be grateful, oftentimes, it will remind you that despite the things you are upset over and are out of your control, you still have a lot to be grateful for, always.

No matter how crazy life gets or little you think you have if you look hard enough, you will find something to be grateful for.

Be grateful for who you are, what you have, who is in your life, and all of the amazing things you will do with it.

Reflect:

Name at least three things you have to be grateful for.

What are things that you may be taking for granted that you should be more grateful for?

Name three people you know or heard of that have it worse than you do.

HELP OTHERS

IF THERE IS one thing that has impacted and changed my life more than anything else, it is helping others. I live my life to make a difference in the world. The joy and happiness it brings is something that happens organically. It fulfills me beyond words.

I am not implying that you must go out and help every person you see or a specific number of people in a particular amount of time. I invite you to consider using your life to make a difference in the world by helping others. Who the others are will be different for everyone. For some, it may be being there for a friend during a breakup, helping a person pick up their groceries after they dropped them, holding the door for someone, or helping a person with his or her homework. There is no one way to help. There are opportunities to help others around you, everyday. You have to stay open to them. Also beyond just helping, never underestimate how much it may mean to the person you help.

I was skateboarding down the sidewalk one day and saw a man sitting on a bench. His name is William. I saw him on the same bench often, but on this particular day, he seemed really down. I felt inspired to ask him if he was okay. It turned out that he was in the process of being evicted from his home and wasn't sure where he would go. After we talked for a bit, I was moved to give him a "You Are Valued" Ripples of Kindness Card. They read "You Are Valued" on the front and "Never stop believing in the greatness of who you are on the back." He looked at the card and started to cry. He said, "I was sitting here on this bench feeling like no one cared. Like giving up." He then went on to tell me how I gave him hope and for him to feel valued meant more to me than I will ever know.

The reality is, by helping someone, you could be saving his or her life. It isn't always about the thing you are helping them with as much as showing them someone cares enough to help. That alone can change someone's life. For some, it could be the very thing that encourages them to keep pushing on when they may feel like giving up. Help who you can where you can.

This is the story of your life. Everything you do will be a part of who you become. Make helping others a part of it, you will be glad you did.

Reflect:

What is an experience you had where you helped someone? How did it make you feel?

Are there people in your life right now who may need your help?

Name three ways that you would feel comfortable helping someone else.

What would the world be like if everyone helped each other in the ways they can?

PURSUE YOUR DREAMS

EVERYONE HAS A dream at some point in his or her life. Things they would like to do. Many have causes they care about. Art they are passionate about. No matter what your dreams are, things you are passionate about, or causes you believe in, nothing happens on its own.

There is a quote I use when I talk with people about pursuing their dreams. It is, "Whatever you vividly imagine, heartedly desire, actively act upon, must inevitably come to pass" (author unknown).

If you imagine it (see it), desire it to be so very deeply and passionately in your heart, act actively upon it with courage and dedication, it will happen.

A woman shared that quote with me years ago at a book signing. She said she lived her life believing it, and it proved to be true. I have also experienced the same truth in my pursuit to inspire others through my books, efforts with *You Are Valued* (Youarevalued.org), and my speaking engagements. It certainly has not been easy, but it is inevitably coming to pass one action at a time.

Nine times out of ten, when I ask what part people are usually missing in regard to pursuing their dreams in relation to the quote, the answer is, "Take action. People don't act on their dreams."

A dream is just a dream if it's not pursued.

Your dreams, passions, and/or the causes you care about, are just dreams, ideas, and beliefs if you don't act on them. The people you see that are living their dreams are doing so because they took action to make them a reality. Things will happen to help you along the way. Opportunities will come. However, they can't and won't come if you are not taking action.

Anything that you desire to do with your life, any dream you have, will require a lot of work. You will face many obstacles. You will be discouraged. You may even feel like giving up, but you must decide to not let any of it stop you from actively acting upon your dreams, and passions. Believe me, I know it's easier said than done. Pursuing your dreams can be scary. There have been times when I have not known where I would live and how I would pay my bills, but things continued to work out. I have felt like giving up more than one time in pursuing my dreams. No matter how afraid I become or discouraged I get, the only way to make my dreams reality is to not only believe in them but to act on them daily and trust that they will inevitably come to pass.

Things don't happen overnight. For example, if you want to become a professional skateboarder, you will have to eventually get sponsored, place well in contests, get coverage, video parts, etc. All of these things take much effort, practice, sacrifice, dedication, courage, and believing. However, none of it will happen without action.

Nothing will just come to you. If you have a dream boiling inside of you, which most people do, go for it. Let it become one of the biggest parts of who you are. Act on it daily. Be patient. Enjoy the many things you will experience along the way.

There is a reason you have the dreams and visions you do. You deserve to make them your reality. The world needs you to!

Reflect:

What are your passions, dreams, and/or causes that you care about?

What are you doing to act on them now?

What is at least one sacrifice you can make that will help you make one of your dreams a reality?

NEVER GIVE UP

I WISH I could tell you that when you get out of school and/or get older than you are now, life will get easy. And if you follow the right path, everything will be smooth sailing. Here is the truth. Life is hard at times. Things will happen that you can't control, and you may wish didn't. People you love will pass away. People will hurt you, lie to you, cheat you, or even on you. You will get rejected. Lose jobs. Make money and lose money. Life will happen, and when it does, you have to happen with it.

Regardless of how tough things get, there are so many more great things that will happen than what we refer to as the bad things. Life is a gift. If you choose, there are always things to be grateful for.

Giving up cannot be an option for you. Can you get discouraged? Yes. Feel like giving up? Absolutely. Get frustrated? Sure. Give up? No way!

No matter what happens in your life, you have to choose to keep trying. It's okay to take breaks. Collect yourself. But don't give up. You can give up on particular jobs, relationships, or even goals you have, when they are no longer in your best interest or are a distraction to you being your best. What I am talking about is giving up on your life, on yourself, on what you have to offer the world. There were many times in my life when I felt like giving up. I felt like my life was not worth living. To others, I seemed so full of life, but I wasn't. I struggled on a daily basis to see the value in who I am and what I have to offer the world. I know life can be tough and how mean some people can be. No matter how much you may feel like giving up at times, please don't. You are so very important and have a great purpose.

> Special Note: If you are feeling like giving up on life, please talk with someone. Ask for help. There are so many people that would love to help you. You are not alone. Also, if you have a friend that makes any comments about giving up on life, please let someone know so they can get the support they deserve.

Never lose sight of making the most and best out of your life. Your life is way too important to every give up on. Shine on!

Reflect:

Have you ever felt like giving up? Why?

What are things you can do to stay encouraged when you do feel like giving up?

Name three reasons why *you* are way to important to ever give up on.

YOU ARE A GIFT
TO THE WORLD

No matter what people say or how many of them do hurtful things to you, how much money you have or don't have, what your home life is like, what adversities and challenges you face, or different abilities (what most people call "disabilities") you have, *you are a gift to this world.*

Years ago, I had the privilege to participate in a community project with a group of young people. We created art to hang in the pediatric unit of a hospital. The project went really well and seemed to be inspiring to everyone involved. At the end of the project, I was asked to give a talk to bring everything together and to leave the group with a message they would remember. I didn't have anything planned. I started to talk in front of the group, thinking "What can I say that will really stick with them?" I saw a mirror in the back of the room. Boom! A lightbulb turned on in my mind. I had an idea! I asked the class if they wanted to see something that is so rare that there is only one in the entire world. They were excited. "Yes," they replied. I invited them to the front of the room. I walked them over to the mirror one by one. When I got them in front of the mirror, I said, "There is nothing better that I can ever show you than yourself. There is only one you in the entire world. Everything you need to succeed is within you."

Think of that. There is only one of you in the entire world, and there will never be another you ever. When I think of that reality, I can't help but to get excited. It's quite special actually. Your uniqueness is a gift! No one can ever take that from you.

You are here for a great purpose. Every one who is given the opportunity to meet you, know you, spend time with you is very fortunate. They are lucky. They will never meet anyone just like you ever again. Even if they don't see it that way it doesn't mean you can't know that about the greatness of who you are. The world would not, and cannot, be what it is if you were not in it. It would be completely different without you because right now, you are a unique piece of the entire population that makes it complete.

Thank you for being here. Thank you for being who you are. Don't change for anyone. Always be you. Stand firm with pride in who you are—a gift to the world.

Reflect:

Write down a list of things that make you a gift to the world.

Please say this out loud: "I am a gift to the world, and there will never be another person just like me!" Now say it again, better yet, find a mirror and read it to yourself in front of it as many times as you want.

CONCLUSION

THANK YOU SO much for reading this book. I truly do hope you enjoyed it. Above all, I hope in some small way it reminds you of the greatness in who you are and what you have to offer the world. As I said in the beginning, I don't have all of the answers. I don't know what it's like to be you, but I do know how important you are.

It was my honor to write this book, knowing I was doing it just for you, the *youth* of our world. I can't make you agree with the things I wrote or even believe in all of the positive things I said about you. The best thing I can do is let you know that I give the biggest part of my life to inspiring youth, *you*. I don't do it for the money or what society thinks of me; I do it because I am passionate about it. It's part of why I am here. There are so many things I wish people would have told me when I was younger, but they didn't. For the ones who tried, they didn't really reach me, and/or I didn't choose to listen to the ways they did try. I firmly believe you can't ever be told enough how special you are and what you have to offer with the gift of your life. I wrote this book because I want the very best for you. However, despite why I wrote it or what my intent for it is, only *you* have the power to choose what you will take away from it and/or what you will do with it.

Whatever you choose to take from the words I have been inspired to share with you, I respect you. I honor you. I trust that you will make the very most out of your life and will do many great things.

You are valued!

I invite you to stay in touch at www.rickyrobertsiii.com and to learn more about You Are Valued at www.youarevalued.org

NOTES

NOTES

RANDOM THOUGHTS

IDEAS

DOODLES

THINGS TO REMEMBER

FINAL THOUGHTS

Made in the USA
Columbia, SC
12 July 2018